SPSS for Students

Copyright

Disclaimer

Although the author has made every effort to ensure that the information in this book is correct, the author
does not assume and hereby disclaims any liability to any party for any loss, damage, or disruption caused by
errors or omissions, whether such errors or omissions result from negligence, accident, or any other cause.

Introduction

If you're reading this, it's quite likely that you're a university student. If so, then you probably have multiple looming deadlines, which are potentially a source of stress and anxiety. The purpose of this book is to reduce or prevent such feelings. It aims to achieve this by teaching you how to complete tests in SPSS quickly and easily, so that writing quantitative reports becomes much more straightforward.

One way in which this text facilitates rapid learning is by assuming that the reader is familiar with various terms that are common to the life sciences. However, don't worry if there's anything that you don't understand; the glossary that is included with this guide provides in-depth definitions of many terms, using examples to improve understanding. Look for words in bold font – they're defined in the glossary. Not sure which test to use? Check immediately below the titles of each section – there are descriptions of what the tests should be used for.

The hypothetical experiments that are described may not always bear much superficial resemblance to the dry examples seen in textbooks (e.g., one group receives a drug, another receives a placebo, and symptoms are measured). This is because experiments needn't be boring. What's important is that the *designs* of the experiments described here – their underlying structures – are identical to those applied in actual research settings.

This guide focuses on parametric tests because, in my years spent tutoring, I've observed that these are far more common than non-parametric tests. However, you should check with your supervisor or lecturer whether parametric tests are appropriate for your data.

I hope you enjoy the book and that you soon feel confident applying SPSS to whatever type of experiment stands before you!

For a Word file containing the data for the exercises, just send me an email (DavidRobinson-Tutor@hotmail.com) with "Data" in the subject line.

David has worked as a life science tutor since 2010, assisting hundreds of students in this time, frequently with SPSS. He completed BSc, MSc, and PhD degrees in psychology and neuroscience while living in and around London, England. He is currently pursuing a career as a scientist, though endeavours to assist students in his spare time. He is also the author of *APA Style and Referencing: The 30+ Most Common Mistakes*, available on Amazon: http://amzn.eu/8XP4UgA

Table of Contents

Independent t-test...5

Paired t-test...9

Independent one-way ANOVA...12

Repeated one-way ANOVA..16

Two-way mixed ANOVA..19

Independent one-way ANCOVA...23

Independent one-way MANOVA..27

Independent one-way MANCOVA..31

Pearson correlation..36

Simple linear regression..39

Multiple linear regression..42

Chi-squared test of independence...45

Thank you!...47

Glossary...48

Independent t-test

When should you use an independent t-test?

Use an independent t-test when you want to compare scores between two groups.

T-tests are some of the simplest analyses you're likely to conduct with SPSS. In the case of *independent* t-tests, they assess whether there's a **significant** difference between the **means** of two groups. For example, say there's a rowing race that has 20 boats competing in it. 10 of the boats race each other in the morning and row in the direction of the tide. The other 10 boats race each other in the afternoon and row against the tide. Every boat receives a time when they've finished. Time, then, is the **dependent variable**. And the **independent variable** is 'tide'. It has two **levels**: 'with' and 'against'. It's pretty obvious that the boats that raced against the tide will tend to be slower than those who raced with the tide. That is, the **mean** time of the 'against' group of boats will be higher than the **mean** time of the 'with'

group of boats. An independent t-test can tell us whether the difference is **significant** – whether the difference is due to the tide, rather than the 'with' group just happening to have superior rowers or boats. Below are the times that each team posted.

Race Times (Seconds) in Different Tide Conditions

With tide	Against tide
132	134
180	133
120	176
125	192
145	144
151	169
172	158
122	149
143	192
131	132

Set up the File

Before entering the data into SPSS, it's necessary to define the variables in Variable View (see the tab at the bottom of the screen). In the top left cell, enter "Tide." Select the cell below the Values tab in the same row. Enter "0" into the Value box, enter "With tide" into the Label box, then click Add. Next, enter "1" in the Value box, enter "Against tide" in the Label box, then click Add, and then OK. Click the cell below the Measure tab and select "**Nominal**." Now that you've told SPSS what the **independent variable** is (Tide) and have specified what its **levels** are (With and Against) you should now indicate what the **dependent variable** is. Select the cell beneath where you entered "Tide" in the Name column, and enter "Time." In the Measure column, specify that Time is a **Scale Variable**.

Enter the Data

You're now ready to enter the data, so click Data View at the bottom of the screen. You should see Tide and Time at the top of the first and second columns, respectively. In the rowing example, there were 10 teams who rowed with the tide, and 10 who rowed against, so 20 teams in total. These 20 teams will be represented by the numbers on the left of the screen. Enter a "0" into each of the cells beside numbers 1–10 in the Tide column, then enter a "1" into each of the cells beside numbers 11–20[1]. You can now enter the data. Copy the data from the With tide column in the table above and paste it into the first 10 cells of the Time column. Copy the data from the Against column and paste it into the 10 cells below.

Run the Analysis

With the data entered, you can run the Independent t-test. In the Analyze menu, select Compare **Means**, then Independent-Samples T Test. In the dialogue box, transfer Time into the Test Variable(s) box, and transfer Tide into the Grouping Variable box. Click on Define Groups, which will open an additional dialogue box. Next to Group 1, enter "0" and next to Group 2, enter "1". Click Continue, then OK, which will start the analysis.

Interpret and Report the Results

From inspecting the **means** in the top table, you can see that the boats that raced with the tide were faster than those who raced against the tide (142.1 seconds on average vs. 157.9 seconds on average). However, the most important value is in the second table in the "Sig. (2- tailed)" column. In this example, the **p-value** is .126. Since this is above .05, there is not a **significant** difference between the groups (i.e., whether boats raced with or against the tide did not **significantly** affect times).

To report the results of this analysis in APA format, you need to identify four values in the top table: the two **means**, and the two **standard deviations** (Std. deviation). You also need to identify three values in the top row of the second table – those in the t column, the **df** (**degrees of freedom**) column, and the **Sig**. (2-tailed) column. In a report, you would write:

An independent-samples t-test was conducted to compare race times in the with tide and against tide conditions. There was not a **significant** difference in times between the with tide

---

[1] If you have "Value Labels" selected in the View menu, the numbers you enter will be translated into descriptions of the **levels** of the variable. E.g., "0" will appear as "Against Tide."

(M = 142.10, SD = 20.63[1]) and against tide (M = 157.90, SD = 23.36) conditions, $t(18)$ = -1.6, p = .126.

---

[1] According to APA guidelines, numbers should usually be rounded to two decimal places. However, this doesn't apply to **p-values**.

Paired t-test

When should you use a paired t-test?

*Use a paired t-test when you want to compare scores between two **conditions** experienced by a single group.*

While **independent-samples** t-tests compare two separate groups in two unique **conditions**, **paired-samples** t-tests compare just one group in two unique **conditions**. For example, you could compare people's ability to walk in a straight line before and after drinking alcohol. Alcohol, then, is the **independent variable**, and

distance is the **dependent variable**. The table below shows how far (in metres) each participant managed to walk on a 10 metre straight line before and after five shots of tequila. You can see that the participants tended not to do as well after a few shots, and a **paired-samples** t-test can tell us whether this difference is **significant**.

Distances (metres) Walked in a Straight Line Before and After Tequila

Before tequila	After tequila
10	7
9	8
10	6
10	9
8	10
9	6
10	10
9	7
10	4
10	1

Set up the File

Enter Variable View (see the tab at the bottom of the screen) in SPSS. For the previous analysis, which was based on an **independent measures** design, the **independent variable** was entered into the top left cell and the Values column was used to specify the different groups (i.e., with or against the tide). However, for **repeated measures** designs, different **levels** of the **independent variable** (in this case, alcohol or no alcohol) are specified in distinct rows and the Value column isn't used. Therefore, enter "Before" into the top left cell and "After" into the cell below it. Use the Measures column to indicate that the data associated with these **levels** (before vs. after) are **scale data** (in this case, distance in metres).

Enter the Data

Enter Data View. Another difference between **independent** and **repeated measures** designs in SPSS is that, with the former, different **levels** of the **independent variable** are on top of each other in a single column, while, with the latter, they're next to each other in separate columns. The data are entered into these columns, thus there is not a separate column for the **dependent variable** like there was in the previous analysis. Note that at the top of the first two columns it says Before and After. Copy and paste the data from the two columns in the table above into the first two columns of SPSS.

Run the Analysis

To run the analysis, go to Analyze, Compare **Means**, and Paired-Samples T Test. In the dialogue box, use the arrow to enter Before into the Variable 1 column and to enter After into the Variable 2 column. Press OK.

Interpret and Report the Results

You'll see in the top table that, after drinking tequila, the participants couldn't walk as far in a straight line; on average, they walked 9.5 metres before, and 6.8 metres after. Looking at the Paired Samples Test table, we can tell whether this difference is **significant**. Looking at the value in the **Sig**. (2–tailed) column, we can see that the difference is **significant** because the value is less than 0.05.

As with the **independent-samples** t-test, to report the result you need to identify the **means** and **standard deviations** for each **condition** in the Paired Sample Statistics table, and the values in the t column, the **df** column, and the **Sig**. 2–tailed column of the Paired Samples Test table. To report these results in APA format, say:

A paired-samples t-test was conducted to compare distance in metres walked in a straight line before and after alcohol consumption. There was a significant difference in distance before (M = 9.50[1], SD = 0.71) and after alcohol consumption (M = 6.80, SD = 2.78), $t(9)$ = 2.73, p = .023.

---

[1] According to APA guidelines, numbers should usually be rounded to two decimal places. However, this doesn't apply to **p-values**.

Independent one-way ANOVA

When should you use an independent one-way ANOVA?

Use an independent one-way ANOVA when you want to compare scores between three of more groups.

A one-way **independent samples** analysis of variance (ANOVA) is similar to an inde**pendent samples** t-test – it compares **means** between groups. However, it should be used when there are three or more **levels** in the **independent variable**. In the **independent-samples** t-test example, there were two **levels** – with and against the tide. For the one-way **independent samples** ANOVA, let's imagine another race, but one with three **levels** in the **independent variable**. For example, let's say there's a 1-kilometre bike race; 10 participants

cycle on a flat course, 10 cycle uphill, and 10 cycle downhill. Look at the times (in seconds) taken to complete the different courses; as expected, those going downhill tend to be faster than those on a flat course, who, in turn, tend to be faster than those going uphill. A one-way **independent samples** ANOVA can be used to investigate whether these differences are **significant**.

Race Times (Seconds) for Different Courses

Flat	Uphill	Downhill
118	104	100
99	156	67
145	178	130
132	183	123
125	143	112
134	110	94
162	199	88
100	157	77
104	159	102
94	166	100

Set up the File

Go to Variable View (see the tab at the bottom of the screen). Into the top left cell, enter the name of the **independent variable**: "Course." Because this is an **independent measures** design, we'll use the Values column to indicate what the **levels** of the **independent variable** are; click on the top cell of the Values column. In the dialogue box, enter "0" into the Value box, enter "Flat" into the Label box, and then click Add. Next, enter "1" in the Value box, enter "Uphill" in the Label box, then click Add. Finally, enter "2" into the Value box, enter "Downhill" in the Label box, then click Add, then OK. Click the top cell in the Measure column and specify that Course is a **nominal variable**. In the second row of the Name column, write Time, and use the corresponding Measure cell to indicate that it is a **scale variable**.

Enter the Data

Go to Data View. In the first column, enter a "0" into each of the cells beside numbers 1-10; enter a "1" into each of the cells beside numbers 11–20; and enter a "2" into each of the cells beside the numbers 21–30[1]. Copy and paste the data from the Flat column in the table

[1] If you have "Value Labels" selected in the View menu, the numbers you enter will be translated into descriptions of the **levels** of the variable. E.g., "0" will appear as "Flat."

13

above into the second column in SPSS next to numbers 1–10. Do the same for the data in the Uphill and Downhill columns, pasting them next to numbers 11–20 and 21–30, respectively.

Run the Analysis

Go to Analyze, General Linear Model, and Univariate. Use the arrows to transfer Course to the Fixed Factor(s) box and Time to the Dependent Variable box. Click Post Hoc, then transfer Course from the Factor(s) box to the Post Hoc Tests for box, then check the Bonferroni box, and then click Continue. Click Options, then check **Descriptive Statistics** and Estimates of effect size, and then click Continue. Click OK.

Interpret and Report the Results

In the **Sig** column of the Tests of Between Subjects Effects table, you can see that the **p-value** in the Course row is .000. Since this is less than .05, the result is **significant**. However, this doesn't tell you whether the **significant** result is attributable to, for example, the difference between uphill and downhill times, or flat and uphill times, etc. The Multiple Comparisons table, which was generated because we previously ticked the Bonferroni box, will provide you with insights into this. By looking at the values in the **Sig** column in the Multiple Comparisons table and at the **means** in the Descriptives table, we can conclude that both the Flat and Downhill groups were **significantly** faster than the Uphill group. However, there was not a **significant** difference between the Flat and Downhill groups (the **p-value** of .161 is higher than .05).

The results of the ANOVA and the Bonferroni can be reported in one paragraph. To report the ANOVA, you need to identify the Course and Error **degrees of freedom (df)**, the Course **F value**, the Course **p-value** (in the **Sig** column), and the Course Partial Eta Squared value (all of which are in the Tests of Between Subjects Effects table). To report the Bonferroni, you just need to refer to the **means** and **standard deviations** (Std. Deviation) in the Descriptives table. The results can be reported in APA format as follows:

A one-way independent-samples analysis of variance (ANOVA) was conducted to investigate the impact of course (Flat, Uphill, Downhill) on race times. There was a significant effect of course on race times, $F(2, 27) = 13.50$, $p < .001$[1], $\eta_p^2 = .50$. Bonferroni post-hoc comparisons revealed that those in the uphill condition ($M = 155.50$, $SD = 30.11$[2]) were significantly slower than those in the flat ($M = 121.30$, $SD = 22.40$) and downhill ($M = 99.30$, $SD = 19.35$) conditions, though there was not a significant difference between those in the downhill and flat conditions.

[1] **P-values** are only shown to three decimal places, thus your actual **p-value** could be any number starting with .000. Therefore, all you know for sure is that the **p-value** is below .001.

[2] According to APA guidelines, numbers should usually be rounded to two decimal places. However, this doesn't apply to **p-values**.

Repeated one-way ANOVA

When should you use a repeated one-way ANOVA?

*Use a repeated one-way ANOVA when you want to compare scores between three or more **conditions** experienced by a single group.*

Imagine that, for one of your classes, you and your peers have three exams spread out evenly over three weeks. The night before the first one, you go out to dinner with each other and most of you get in around 23.00. The night before the second one, you all decide to stay in and get an early night. The night before the third exam, you decide to go out for a drink and most of you don't get home until  the sun's up. Assuming the exams are equally difficult, you might guess that you and your peers perform worst on the third exam, best on the second exam, and somewhere in between on the first. Since this "experiment" uses a **repeated measures** design and the one **categorical independent variable** has more than two **levels**[1], you can explore this hypothesis by using a one-way **repeated measures** analysis of variance (ANOVA). The percentages that you and your nine classmates got in each of the exams are in the table below.

---

[1] If the **independent variable** only had two **levels**, you'd use a paired t-test.

Results (%) for Different Exams

1st exam	2nd exam	3rd exam
65	71	70
70	72	60
43	48	30
47	45	45
63	62	55
31	48	45
80	81	70
45	55	56
61	68	55
67	69	61

Set up the File

Since this is a **repeated measures** design, in Variable View (see the tab at the bottom of the screen) you'll need separate rows for each of **level** of the **independent variable**. Enter "First_Exam"[1] into the top left cell, "Second_Exam" into the cell below it, and "Third_Exam" into the third cell down. In the Measures column, indicate that you're using **Scale data**.

Enter the Data

Enter Data View. Note that the first three columns are labelled with the **levels** of the **independent variable** (First_Exam, etc.). Copy the data from the table above, and paste them into SPSS.

Run the Analysis

To analyse the data, go to Analyze, General Linear Model, and Repeated Measures. In the Within-Subject Factor Name box enter Exam. In the Number of Levels box, enter a "3" and click Add, then Define. Transfer the three **levels** of the **independent variable** (First_Exam,

[1] Spaces aren't permitted in these cells, hence the underscore.

etc.) into the Within-Subjects Variables box. Click Options, tick **Descriptive Statistics** and Estimates of effect size, then click Continue. Click OK.

Interpret and Report the Results

In the **Descriptive Statistics** table in the output you can see that the **mean** percentages correspond to the hypothesis that scores would be highest for the second exam (61.9), lowest for the third exam (53.7), and that scores for the first exam would be somewhere in between (57.2).

To determine whether these differences are **significant**, look at the Tests of Within-Subjects Effects table. Look for the top value in the Sig column; in this case, it's .009, so the scores for the different exams differed **significantly** from each other. To report this, you need to identify the **degrees of freedom (df)**, **F-value**, **p-value (Sig)**, and Partial Eta Squared values in the top row of the Tests of Within-Subjects Effects table, and the **df** value in the 5th row down. Report the statistics (in APA format) like this:

A one-way repeated-samples analysis of variance (ANOVA) was conducted to investigate the impact of pre-exam activity on exam performance. There was a significant effect of pre-exam activity on exam performance, $F(2, 18) = 6.22$[1], $p = .009$, $\eta_p^2 = .41$.

Note that the test only informs us that the pre-exam activities **significantly** affected exam performance, but does not indicate whether, for example, the scores on the first exam **significantly** differed from the scores on the second exam, or whether the scores on the third exam differed from the scores on the first and second exams. Therefore, **paired-samples** t-tests would be required to look into this (see page 8). If the **Sig value** had been above 0.05 (i.e., not **significant**), further tests would not be conducted.

---

[1] According to APA guidelines, numbers should usually be rounded to two decimal places. However, this doesn't apply to **p-values**.

Two-way mixed ANOVA

When should you use a two-way mixed ANOVA?

*Use a two-way mixed ANOVA when you want to compare scores between two or more groups, as well as between two or more **conditions** experienced by single groups (i.e., when your design has **independent** and **repeated** elements).*

The tests covered so far – t-tests and one-way ANOVAs – are used to investigate the effect of a single **independent categorical variable** on a **dependent variable**. However, there are times when it's interesting to look at the influence of multiple **independent categorical variables** on a **dependent variable**. In such cases, one can use two-way ANOVAs, the most common of which is a two-way mixed <u>an</u>alysis <u>of</u> <u>var</u>iance (ANOVA). "Two-way" refers to there being two **independent variables**[1]; "mixed" refers to an experimental design that has **within-** and **between-participant** components. For instance, say there are two groups of monkeys – males and females. Both eat fruit, but the males are fatter so tend to eat more

pieces per day than the females. Also, you suspect that the males prefer red fruits, while the females prefer yellow fruits. So, while the males might eat a greater number of fruits per day, this effect might be minimised when the monkeys are given yellow fruits and exaggerated when they're given red fruits. This is known as an **interaction**. This can be investigated with a two-way mixed ANOVA, where the **between-participant** variable is sex, and the **within-participant** variable is fruit colour.

---

[1] It's possible to apply ANOVAs to experiments that have more than two **independent variables**. However, the steps required to run such tests are the same as for a two-way ANOVA, so ANOVAs with more than two **independent variables** are not covered here.

Number of Red and Yellow Fruits Eaten by Males and Females

Males		Females	
Red	Yellow	Red	Yellow
20	17	11	15
18	15	13	16
17	14	10	14
23	16	12	15
26	13	9	14
19	15	8	13
15	14	13	17
17	16	14	15
19	18	13	13
19	11	12	14

Set up the File

Go to Variable View (see the tab at the bottom of the screen) and enter "Sex" into the top left cell. Click on the corresponding cell under Values and enter "0" into the Value box, then "Male" into the Label box and click Add. Enter "1" into the Value box, then "Female" into the Label box and click Add, then OK. Use the Measure column to indicate that Sex is a **nominal variable**. In the cell below where you've written Sex, enter "Red_fruit"[1], and "Yellow_fruit" into the cell below that. In the second and third cells of the Measure column select **Scale**.

Enter the Data

Go to Data View. Enter "0"s into the first 10 cells of the Sex column, and "1"s into the next 10 cells[2]. Copy the males' data from the table above and paste them next to the 0s in SPSS. Copy the females' data and paste them next to the 1s in SPSS. You're now ready to run the analysis.

---

[1] Spaces aren't permitted in these cells, hence the underscore.

[2] If you have "Value Labels" selected in the View menu, the numbers you enter will be translated into descriptions of the **levels** of the variable. E.g., "0" will appear as "Male."

Run the Analysis

Go to Analyze, General Linear Model, and Repeated Measures. In the Within-Subject Factor Name box enter Fruit_colour, enter "2" into the Number of Levels box, click Add, and then Define. Transfer Sex into the Between-Subject Factor(s) box, then Red_fruit, followed by Yellow_fruit, into the Within-Subjects Variables box. Click Options, then transfer Sex and Fruit_colour from the Factor(s) and Factor Interactions box to the Display **Means** for box, tick **Descriptive Statistics** and Estimates of effect size, then click Continue, then OK.

Interpret and Report the Results

Look at the Tests of Within-Subjects Effects table. The top **Sig value** of .341 indicates that, when sex is disregarded, there was not a **significant** difference between the number of red and yellow pieces of fruit consumed. However, the fifth **Sig value** down (.000) indicates that there was a significant **interaction** between fruit colour and sex (i.e., how much fruit of a given colour was consumed depends upon sex). In the **Descriptive Statistics** table, you can see that males at much more red fruit than the females, though there was little difference between males and females with regard to how much yellow fruit they consumed. In the Tests of Between-Subjects Effects table, the **Sig value** in the Sex row (.000) indicates that, when colour is disregarded, sex had a **significant** impact on how much was eaten. In the Sex table, you can see that males ate more fruit overall than females. These results can be reported (in APA format) like this:

A two-way mixed analysis of variance (ANOVA) was conducted to investigate the impact of sex and fruit colour on fruit consumption. There was not a significant main effect of fruit colour, $F(1, 18) = .96$[1], $p = .341$, $\eta_p^2 = .05$[2]. However, there was a significant main effect of sex, $F(1, 18) = 30.68$, $p < .001$[3], $\eta_p^2 = .64$, with males ($M = 17.10$) consuming more fruit overall than females ($M = 13.05$). Additionally, there was a significant interaction between sex and fruit colour, $F(1, 18) = 31.78$, $p < .001$, $\eta_p^2 = .64$.

[1] According to APA guidelines, numbers should usually be rounded to two decimal places. However, this doesn't apply to **p-values**.

[2] η_p^2 values are shown in the Partial Eta Squared columns.

[3] **P-values** are only shown to three decimal places, thus your actual **p-value** could be any number starting with .000. Therefore, all you know for sure is that the **p-value** is below .001.

It's conventional to follow up significant **interactions** with t-tests. For example, you might want to know whether males eat **significantly** more red fruit than yellow fruit, or whether females eat **significantly** more yellow fruit than red fruit. Also, you could look into whether males eat **significantly** more red fruit than females, or whether there's a difference in yellow fruit consumption between males and females. The last of these two questions are easy to answer; you would just do two independent t-tests as described in the first section of this guide. For the first of the above two questions you need to tell SPSS to look at the data for males and females separately. To do this, go to Data, than Split File. Select Organize output by groups, transfer Sex to the Groups Based on box, then click OK. You then just need to run a paired t-test as described in the second section of this guide. Refer to pages 7 and 10 to see how to report the results of independent and paired t-tests.

Independent one-way ANCOVA

When should you use an independent one-way ANCOVA?

*Use an independent one-way ANCOVA when you want to compare scores between two or more groups while controlling for **covariates**.*

An <u>analysis</u> <u>of</u> <u>covariance</u> ANCOVA is like an ANOVA – it compares **means** between groups – but it can also control for other factors. In the one-way ANOVA section we compared times taken to complete a bike race when participants raced uphill, downhill, or on a flat surface. It was concluded that those in the uphill **condition** were slower than those in who

raced on a flat surface or downhill. However, let's suppose that the researcher – for some reason – wanted to exaggerate the differences in the race times between the three groups. Accordingly, they chose participants with the most racing experience to be in the downhill group and those with the least to be in the uphill group (of course, an honest researcher would normally allocate participants to groups randomly). The table from the one-way ANOVA section is shown below, though now also includes columns that describe how many years' racing experience each participant has.

Experience (Years) and Race Times (Seconds) for Different Courses

Flat		Uphill		Downhill	
Experience	Race times	Experience	Race times	Experience	Race times
4	118	3	104	7	100
5	99	2	156	9	67
3	145	4	178	8	130
7	132	1	183	6	123
4	125	3	143	7	112
5	134	2	110	7	94
5	162	3	199	8	88
4	100	1	157	8	77
5	104	2	159	7	102
6	94	2	166	6	100

Set up the File

Go to Variable View (see the tab at the bottom of the screen). Into the top left cell, enter the name of the **independent variable**: "Course." Because this is an **independent measures** design, we'll use the Values column to indicate what the **levels** of the **independent variable** are; click on the top cell of the Values column. In the dialogue box, enter "0" into the Value box, enter "Flat" into the Label box, and then click Add. Next, enter "1" into the Value box, enter "Uphill" into the Label box, then click Add. Finally, enter "2" into the Value box, enter "Downhill" into the Label box, then click Add, then OK. Click the top cell in the Measure column and specify that Course is a **nominal variable**. In the second row of the Name column, write Time, and use the corresponding Measure cell to indicate that it is a **scale variable**. Lastly, enter Experience into the third row of the Name column and use the corresponding Measure cell to indicate that it is a **scale variable**.

Enter the Data

Go to Data View. In the first column, enter a "0" into each of the cells beside numbers 1-10; enter a "1" into each of the cells beside numbers 11–20; and enter a "2" into each of the cells beside numbers 21–30[1]. Copy and paste the race times from the Flat column in the table above into the second column in SPSS next to numbers 1–10. Do the same for the race times in the Uphill and Downhill columns, pasting them next to numbers 11–20 and 21–30, respectively. Copy and paste the data from the left-most Exp. (years) column into the third column in SPPS next to numbers 1–10. Do the same for the data in the middle and right-most Exp. (years) columns, pasting them next to numbers 11–20 and 21–30, respectively.

Run the Analysis

Go to Analyze, General Linear Model, Univariate. In the window that opens, transfer Time to the **Dependent Variable** box, Course to the Fixed Factor(s) box, and Experience to the Covariate(s) box. Click Options, check **Descriptive Statistics** and Estimates of effect size, then click Continue, and then OK.

Interpret and Report the Results

Look at the Tests of Between-Subjects Effects table. Specifically, look at the **Sig value** in the Course row. In contrast to the output from the independent one-way ANOVA, in this output the **Sig value**, which is above .05, does not indicate that race times were **significantly** different between the groups; the effect of course is not **significant** when controlling for levels of experience between groups. To report the results, you also need to locate the **df** values in the Course and Error rows, as well as the F value and Partial Eta Squared value in the Course row. The result can be reported (in APA format) like this:

A one-way between groups analysis of covariance (ANCOVA) was conducted to investigate the impact of course (Flat, Uphill, Downhill) on race times. Participants' years of racing

---

[1] If you have "Value Labels" selected in the View menu, the numbers you enter will be translated into descriptions of the **levels** of the variable. E.g., "0" will appear as "Flat."

experience were used as a covariate. There was no significant effect of course on race times, $F(2, 26) = 1.04^{1}$, $p = .366$, $\eta_p^2 = .07$.

Note that, because there was not a **significant** relationship between course type and race times, no further tests are required. However, had there been a **significant** effect of course type, independent t-tests would be used to investigate whether race times differed between the uphill and flat courses, the uphill and downhill courses, and the flat and downhill courses.

---

[1] According to APA guidelines, numbers should usually be rounded to two decimal places. However, this doesn't apply to **p-values**.

Independent one-way MANOVA

When should you use an independent one-way MANOVA?

*Use an independent one-way MANOVA when you want to compare scores on two or more **dependent variables** between two or more groups.*

Often, it's possible to measure something in more than one way. For example, we might be interested in academic performance, which, of course, could be assessed by a multitude of tests, such as exams that measure one's mastery of mathematics or English. In this case, mathematics and English exams assess performance in different areas, but both could be used to measure a more generable **dependent variable** – academic performance.

Let's say that we're interested in how hydration affects academic performance. We could set up an experiment that has two groups – a well hydrated group and a dehydrated group. Thus, our **independent variable** – hydration – has two **levels** – hydrated and dehydrated. We could give each group a 10-question mathematics test and a 10-question English

test; our **dependent variables**, therefore, are mathematics and English performance, which are components of a more general **dependent variable** – academic performance. Since we have separate groups of participants (hydrated and dehydrated), one **independent variable** (hydration), and multiple **dependent variables** (English and mathematics scores), our data can be analysed with a one-way independent multivariate analysis of variance (MANOVA).

Set up the File

Use the tab at the bottom of SPSS to enter Variable View. In the top left cell enter "Hydration," then click on the corresponding cell in the Values column. In the Value box enter "0" then type "Hydrated" in the label box, and then click Add. Next, enter a "1" into the Value box, then type "Dehydrated" into the label box, then click Add, and then OK. Type

"Mathematics" into the cell below Hydration and "English" into the cell below Mathematics. Finally, use the Measures column to indicate that Hydration is a **Nominal variable** and that both Mathematics and English scores are **Ordinal variables**.

Enter the Data

Go to Data View. You should see that Hydration, Mathematics, and English have appeared above the first three columns. Enter a "0" into the first 10 cells of the Hydration column (next to numbers 1–10) and a "1" into the next 10 cells (next to numbers 11–20)[1]. Copy the mathematics and English scores for the 10 hydrated participants from the table below and paste them into the second and third columns of SPSS (next to numbers 1–10). Next, copy the mathematics and English scores for the 10 dehydrated participants from the table below and paste them into the second and third columns of SPSS (next to numbers 11–20).

Mathematics and English Test Scores in Hydrated and Dehydrated Groups

Hydrated		Dehydrated	
Mathematics	English	Mathematics	English
10	8	7	8
9	7	5	5
7	9	6	6
8	6	3	3
5	8	4	5
7	10	6	2
8	8	5	7
7	9	7	5
6	7	5	4
7	6	4	3

[1] If you have "Value Labels" selected in the View menu, the numbers you enter will be translated into descriptions of the **levels** of the variable. E.g., "0" will appear as "Hydrated."

Run the Analysis

Once you've entered the data, you're ready to run the analysis. Go to Analyze, then General Linear Model, and then Multivariate. Transfer Mathematics and English into the **Dependent Variables** box and Hydration into the Fixed Factor(s) box. Click on Options, tick **Descriptive Statistics** and Estimates of effect size, click Continue, and then OK.

Interpret and Report the Results

To determine whether hydration had a **significant** impact on general academic performance, look at the Multivariate Tests table. We can ignore the numbers in the Value column, which leaves us with the numbers in the five remaining columns; you'll notice that the numbers in these columns are the same in each row, so it doesn't matter which row you look at. We can also overlook the numbers in the top half of the table (next to Intercept). Since the **Sig value** in the bottom half of the table (.001) is below .05, we can conclude that hydration had a **significant** impact on academic performance. When we come to report the results, we'll need, in addition to the **Sig value**, the **F**, Hypothesis **df**, and Error **df**, and Partial Eta Squared values.

Having established that hydration had a **significant** impact on general academic performance, we can now look at the Tests of Between-Subjects Effects table to see whether it also affects mathematics and/or English performance individually. We're primarily interested in the numbers in the Hydration section of the table (the third set of rows down). From inspecting the **Sig values** for mathematics (.002) and English (.001), we can see that hydration had a **significant** impact on performance in both exams. The **means** in the **Descriptive Statistics** table indicate that test scores for both mathematics and English were higher in the hydrated group. When reporting the results, we'll need to present these **means**, as well as the **standard deviations** (in the same table). Moreover, in addition to the **Sig values**, we'll also need the **df**, **F**, and Partial Eta Squared values in the Hydration section of the Tests of Between-Subjects Effects table, as well as the **df** values in the Error section of the same table.

The results can be reported in APA format as follows:

A one-way independent multivariate analysis of variance (MANOVA) was conducted to investigate the impact of hydration on academic performance (mathematics and English). There was a significant impact of hydration on academic performance, $F(2, 17) = 11.78$[1], $p = .001$, $\eta_p^2 = .58$. Univariate analyses indicated that hydration had a significant impact on performance in both mathematics, $F(1, 18) = 12.81$, $p = .002$, $\eta_p^2 = .42$, and English, $F(1, 18) = 17.16$, $p = .001$, $\eta_p^2 = .49$. Exam scores in the hydrated condition for mathematics ($M = 7.40$, $SD = 1.43$) and English ($M = 7.80$, $SD = 1.32$) were higher than the mathematics ($M = 5.20$, $SD = 1.32$) and English ($M = 4.80$, $SD = 1.87$) exam scores in the dehydrated condition.

[1] According to APA guidelines, numbers should usually be rounded to two decimal places. However, this doesn't apply to **p-values**.

Independent one-way MANCOVA

When should you use an independent one-way MANCOVA?

*Use an independent one-way MANCOVA when you want to compare scores on two or more **dependent variables** between two or more groups while controlling for **covariates**.*

As described in the previous section, it's often possible to measure something in more than one way. For instance, we might be interested in academic performance, which can be assessed in many ways, such as with mathematics or English exams. These two exam types assess performance in different areas, but both measure a more generable **dependent variable** – academic performance.

As per the example in the previous section, let's again imagine that we're interested in how hydration affects academic performance. We could set up an experiment that has two groups – a well hydrated group and a dehydrated group. Thus, our **independent variable** – hydration – has two **levels** – hydrated and dehydrated. We could give each group a 10-question mathematics test and a 10-question English test; our **dependent variables**, therefore, are mathematics and English performance, which are components of a more general **dependent variable** – academic performance.

In the example in the one-way independent MANOVA section, we concluded that hydration had a **significant** impact on academic performance. However, it's possible that another variable – that we didn't account for – also affects academic performance. For instance, perhaps those in the well hydrated **condition** had simply gotten more sleep. We can use a one-way independent multivariate analysis of covariance (MANCOVA) to assess whether hydration has a **significant** impact on academic performance after accounting for a **covariate** – the hours for which participants slept before the exams.

A one-way independent MANCOVA is appropriate because we have separate groups of participants (hydrated and dehydrated), one **independent variable** (hydration), multiple **dependent variables** (English and mathematics scores), and a **covariate** (hours for which participants slept before the exams).

Set up the File

Use the tab at the bottom of SPSS to enter Variable View. In the top left cell enter "Hydration," then click on the corresponding cell in the Values column. In the Value box enter "0" then type "Hydrated" in the label box, and then click Add. Next, enter a "1" into the Value box, then type "Dehydrated" into the label box, then click Add, and then OK. Type "Mathematics" into the cell below Hydration; type "English" into the cell below Mathematics; and type "Hours_slept"[1] into the cell below English. Finally, use the Measures column to indicate that Hydration is a **Nominal variable**, that both Mathematics and English scores are **Ordinal variables**, and that Hours_slept is a **scale variable**.

Enter the Data

Go to Data View. You should see that Hydration, Mathematics, English, and Hours_slept have appeared above the first four columns. Enter a "0" into the first 10 cells of the Hydration column (next to numbers 1–10) and a "1" into the next 10 cells (next to numbers 11–20)[2]. Copy the mathematics and English scores, as well as the sleep data, for the 10 hydrated participants from the table below and paste it into the second, third, and fourth columns of SPSS (next to numbers 1–10). Next, copy the mathematics and English scores, as well as the sleep data, for the 10 dehydrated participants from the table below and paste it into the second, third, and fourth columns of SPSS (next to numbers 11–20).

[1] Spaces aren't permitted in these cells, hence the underscore.

[2] If you have "Value Labels" selected in the View menu, the numbers you enter will be translated into descriptions of the **levels** of the variable. E.g., "0" will appear as "Hydrated."

Mathematics and English Test Scores, and Hours Slept, in Hydrated and Dehydrated Groups

Hydrated			Dehydrated		
Mathematics	English	Sleep	Mathematics	English	Sleep
10	8	8	7	8	6
9	7	7	5	5	4
7	9	9	6	6	5
8	6	6	3	3	6
5	8	5	4	5	3
7	10	6	6	2	5
8	8	7	5	7	8
7	9	6	7	5	5
6	7	7	5	4	4
7	6	7	4	3	5

Run the Analysis

Once you've entered the data, you're ready to run the analysis. Go to Analyze, then General Linear Model, and then Multivariate. Transfer Mathematics and English into the **Dependent Variables** box, Hydration into the Fixed Factor(s) box, and Hours_slept into the Covariate(s) box. Click on Options, tick **Descriptive Statistics** and Estimates of effect size, Continue, and then OK.

Interpret and Report the Results

To determine whether hydration had a **significant** impact on general academic performance after accounting for hours slept, look at the Multivariate Tests table. We can ignore the numbers in the Value column, which leaves us with the numbers in the five remaining columns. Since the **Sig value** in the bottom third of the table (.017) is below .05, we can conclude that hydration had a **significant** impact on academic performance after accounting for hours slept. Also, since the **Sig value** in the Hours_slept section of the table (.389) is above .05, we can conclude that the number of hours for which participants slept before the exams didn't have a **significant** effect on overall academic performance. When we come to report these results, we'll need, in addition to the **Sig values**, the **F**, Hypothesis **df**, Error **df**, and Partial Eta Squared values.

Having established that hydration has a **significant** impact on general academic performance, we can now look at the Tests of Between-Subjects Effects table to see whether it also affects mathematics and/or English performance individually. We're primarily interested in the numbers in the Hydration section of the table (the fourth set of rows down). From inspecting the **Sig values** for mathematics (.037) and English (.013), we can see that hydration had a **significant** impact on performance in both exams after factoring in sleep. Since we have already established – from inspecting the Multivariate Tests table – that sleep didn't have a **significant** effect on overall academic performance, we can ignore the Hours_slept section of the Tests of Between-Subjects Effects table.

The **means** in the **Descriptive Statistics** table indicate that test scores for both mathematics and English were higher in the hydrated group. When reporting the results, we'll need to present these **means**, as well as the **standard deviations** (in the same table). Moreover, in addition to the **Sig values**, we'll also need the **df**, **F**, and Partial Eta Squared values in the Hydration section of the Tests of Between-Subjects Effects table, as well as the **df** values in the Error section of the same table.

The results can be reported in APA format as follows:

A one-way independent multivariate analysis of covariance (MANCOVA) was conducted to investigate the impact of hydration on academic performance (mathematics and English). The number of hours for which participants slept before the experiment was added as a covariate. There was a significant impact of hydration on academic performance, $F(2, 16) = 5.3$, $p = .017$, $\eta_p^2 = .40$. Conversely, sleep did not have a significant effect on academic performance, $F(2, 16) = 1$, $p = .389$, $\eta_p^2 = .11$. Univariate analyses indicated that hydration had a significant impact on performance in both mathematics, $F(1, 17) = 5.11$[1], $p = .037$, $\eta_p^2 = $

---

[1] According to APA guidelines, numbers should usually be rounded to two decimal places. However, this doesn't apply to **p-values**.

.23, and English, $F(1, 17) = 7.77$, $p = .013$, $\eta_p^2 = .31$. Exam scores in the hydrated condition for mathematics ($M = 7.40$, $SD = 1.43$) and English ($M = 7.80$, $SD = 1.32$) were higher than the mathematics ($M = 5.20$, $SD = 1.32$) and English ($M = 4.80$, $SD = 1.87$) exam scores in the dehydrated condition.

Pearson correlation

When should you use Pearson correlation?

*Use Pearson correlation to test whether there is a **linear relationship** between two scores in a single group.*

A Pearson product-moment correlation coefficient can be used to assess the degree to which two **ordinal** or **scale** variables are **linearly associated** with each other. Put simply, as

one variable increases, does another also increase or decrease? For instance, say you were interested in how lack of sleep affects driving, you could look at whether there's a relationship between how much sleep participants have and how many errors they make on a driving simulator. In this example you would expect there to be a **negative**

correlation (i.e., as one variable increases [hours of sleep], the other decreases [number of driving errors]). The data in the table below appears to support this hypothesis. A Pearson product-moment correlation coefficient can be calculated to determine whether this apparent relationship is **significant**.

Sleep Duration (Hours) and Number of Driving Errors

Sleep Duration	Driving errors
1	17
2	15
3	15
4	13
5	14
6	11
7	8
8	5
9	6
10	4

Set up the File

Go to Variable View (see the tab at the bottom of the screen) and enter "Hours_Sleep"[1] into the top left cell and "No_Driving_Errors" into the cell below, then, in the Measure column, indicate that both variables are **Scale**.

Enter the Data

Go to Data View. Copy and paste the data from the table above into the top of the first two columns.

Run the Analysis

To analyse the data, go to Analyze, Correlate, and Bivariate. In the window that opens, transfer the variables into the Variables box. The Pearson test is the default (note that it's already selected), so you can just click OK.

[1] Spaces aren't permitted in these cells, hence the underscore.

Interpret and Report the Results

In the output you can see that there is a Pearson correlation value of -.966. The minus sign indicates that there is a **negative correlation** between the two variables. Pearson coefficients can be between -1 and 1. A value that's close to -1 indicates a strong **negative correlation**, while a value that's close to 1 indicates a strong **positive correlation**. You can also see that the **Sig value** is .000 (or lower), so the correlation is **significant**. These results can be reported (in APA format) as follows:

A Pearson product-moment correlation coefficient was computed to assess the relationship between hours of sleep and number of driving errors. There was a significant negative correlation between the two variables, $r = .97$[1], $p < .001$[2].

---

[1] According to APA guidelines, numbers should usually be rounded to two decimal places. However, this doesn't apply to **p-values**.

[2] **P-values** are only shown to three decimal places, thus your actual **p-value** could be any number starting with .000. Therefore, all you know for sure is that the **p-value** is below .001.

Simple linear regression

When should you use simple linear regression?

Use simple linear regression to test whether scores associated with one measure can predict scores associated with another measure.

Simple linear regression is similar to correlation in that it allows you investigate the **linear relationship** between variables (e.g., as height increases, does shoe size also?). However,

regression analyses also provide you with a formula that allows you to predict a score on one variable based on a score of another variable. For instance, we might predict that there's a **linear relationship** between how far a student lives from university (the predictor variable) and how often they're late for lectures (the criterion variable); with a greater distance and with potentially more forms of transport required, there are more opportunities for delays. The formula derived from a simple regression analysis would allow us to predict how many times someone will be late in a given time period based on where they live and vice versa. From the table below, you can see that the further a student lives from campus, the more often they're late per year.

Distance from Campus (Miles) and Times Late to Lectures

Distance from campus	Times late to lectures
1	3
7	18
15	37
3	10
2	6
2	8
6	23
4	17
9	25
1	2

Set up the File

In Variable View (see the tab at the bottom of the screen), enter "Distance" into the top left cell, and "Times_Late"[1] into the one below it. Use the Measure column to indicate that we're using **Scale data**.

Enter the Data

Copy the data from the Distance from campus (miles) and Times late to lectures per year columns in the table above, and paste it into the top of the two left-most columns in Data View.

Run the Analysis

To run the analysis, go to Analyze, Regression, and then Linear. In the window that opens, transfer Times_late to the Dependent box and Distance to the Independent box, then click OK.

[1] Spaces aren't permitted in these cells, hence the underscore.

Interpret and Report the Results

Firstly, look at the R Square column of the Model Summary table. This indicates how much of the variation your model explains. I.e., the distance someone lives from campus can be used to explain 93% of variation in lateness to lectures, which is a lot. The ANOVA table below it indicates whether the model predicts a **significant** amount of variation; when reporting the results, in addition to the R Square value, you'll need to know the **df** values in the Regression and Residual rows, as well as the **F** and **Sig values**. You'll also need a few of the stats from the Coefficients table; the B value, the t value, and the **Sig value** in the Distance row. The results can be reported (in APA format) like this:

Simple linear regression was used to assess whether distance from campus significantly predicts arriving late to lectures. The results of the regression suggested that distance from campus explained 93% of the variance, $r^2 = .93$[1], $F(1, 8) = 107.29$, $p < .001$[2]. Distance from campus significantly predicted arriving late to lectures, $b = 2.44$, $t = 10.36$, $p < .001$.

Note that the numbers in the Coefficients table can be used to predict how often someone will be late for lectures per year on the basis of how far from the campus they live. To do this, you multiply the B value in the Distance row by the number of miles a person lives from campus and add this to the B value in the Constant row. For example, if someone lives five miles from campus: 5 X 2.44 = 12.2 and 12.2 + 2.68 = 14.88. So, the model predicts that, if someone lives five miles from campus, they'd be late about 15 times per year.

[1] According to APA guidelines, numbers should usually be rounded to two decimal places. However, this doesn't apply to **p-values**.

[2] **P-values** are only shown to three decimal places, thus your actual **p-value** could be any number starting with .000. Therefore, all you know for sure is that the **p-value** is below .001.

Multiple linear regression

When should you use multiple linear regression?

Use multiple linear regression to test whether scores associated with two or more measures can predict scores associated with another measure.

As with simple linear regression, multiple linear regression is used to investigate the **linear relationships** between variables. However, while simple linear regression uses a single

predictor variable, multiple linear regression uses two more or predictor variables. In the last example, we used simple linear regression to assess the relationship between how far someone lives from campus (predictor variable) and how often they're late to lectures (criterion variable). The former explained 93% of the variance in the latter.

While this is excellent, it's possible that, by using an additional predictor variable, we could explain even more of the variance. For instance, we might also factor in how far people live from the nearest train station. See the table below.

Distance from Campus (Miles) and Closest Train Station (Miles) and Times Late to Lectures

Distance from campus	Distance from closest train station	Times late to lectures
1	1	3
7	4	18
15	10	37
3	4	10
2	1	6
2	3	8
6	7	23
4	6	17
9	8	25
1	1	2

Set up the File

In Variable View (see the tab at the bottom of the screen), enter "Distance_campus"[1] into the top left cell, "Distance_station" into the cell below it, and "Times_late" into the third cell down. Use the Measures column to indicate that we're using **Scale data**.

Enter the Data

Go to Data view. Copy the data from table above and paste them into the top of the three left-most columns.

Run the Analysis

To run the analysis, go to Analyze, Regression, and then Linear. In the window that opens, transfer Times_late to the Dependent box and Distance_campus and Distance_station to the Independent box, then click OK.

[1] Spaces aren't permitted in these cells, hence the underscore.

Interpret and Report the Results

Firstly, look at the R Square column of the Model Summary table. This indicates how much of the variation your model explains. I.e., one's distance from campus and from their nearest train station can explain 99% (.986 rounded up) of the variation in lateness to lectures. Note that this figure is higher than when we only had one predictor variable (distance from campus) in the Simple Linear Regression section, so one's distance from their nearest train station contributes to the predictive power of the model. The ANOVA table indicates whether the model predicts a **significant** amount of variation; when reporting the results, in addition to the R Square value, you'll need to know the **df** values in the Regression and Residual rows, as well as the **F** and **Sig values**. You'll also need a few of the stats from the Coefficients table; the B, t, and **Sig values** in the Distance_campus and Distance_station rows. The results can be reported (in APA format) like this:

Multiple regression analysis was used to assess whether a student's distance from campus and from their nearest train station significantly predict arriving late to lectures. The results of the regression suggested that distance from campus and distance from nearest train station explained 99% of the variance, $r^2 = .99$[1], $F(2, 7) = 241.86$, $p < .001$[2]. Distance from campus ($b = 1.25$, $t = 4.86$, $p = .002$) and distance from nearest train station ($b = 1.86$, $t = 5.20$, $p = .001$) both significantly predicted arriving late to lectures.

As with the simple linear regression, the numbers in the multiple linear regression output can be used to predict how often someone will be late to lectures per year on the basis of their distance from the campus and their nearest station. For example, let's say that someone lives 10 miles from the university and 5 miles from their nearest station. We multiply these numbers by the B values in the Coefficients table: 10 X 1.25 = 12.5 and 5 X 1.86 = 9.3. Next, we add these values together and add the total to the B value in the Constant column: 12.5 + 9.3 + .28 = 22.08. So we'd expect this person to be late about 22 times per year.

[1] According to APA guidelines, numbers should usually be rounded to two decimal places. However, this doesn't apply to **p-values**.

[2] **P-values** are only shown to three decimal places, thus your actual **p-value** could be any number starting with .000. Therefore, all you know for sure is that the **p-value** is below .001.

Chi-squared test of independence

When should you use a chi-squared test of independence?

*Use a chi-squared test of independence to test whether an event is more frequent in one **condition** compared to another.*

If you want to test whether certain events happen more frequently under certain **conditions**, you can do this with a chi-squared test of independence. For example, it would

be reasonable to guess that people in a relatively cold country (e.g., Scotland) are more likely to wear jackets than t-shirts, and that people in a relatively hot country (e.g., Spain) are more likely to wear t-shirts than jackets. Two researchers – one in Scotland, one in Spain – could keep a tally of how often they see each type of clothing. Once they've each noted what 20 people are wearing they stop; see the results in the contingency table below. There appears to be a clear difference in the type of clothing worn in each country; a chi-squared test of

independence can determine whether this difference is **significant**.

Number of People Wearing T-shirts or Jackets in Different Countries

	T-shirts	Jackets
Scotland	4	16
Spain	13	7

Set up the File

Go to Variable View (see the tab at the bottom of the screen). Enter "Country" into the top left cell and "Clothing" into the cell below, then use the Measures column to indicate that they're **nominal variables**. Click on the cell in the Values column that corresponds to Country. Enter a "0" into the Value box and write "Scotland" in the label box, then click Add. Next, enter a "1" into the Value box and write "Spain" in the label box, then click Add, then OK. Click on the cell in the Values column that corresponds to Clothing. Enter a "0" into the

Value box and write "T-shirt" in the label box, then click Add. Next, enter a "1" into the Value box and write "Jacket" in the label box, then click Add, then OK.

Enter the Data

Go to Data View. In the left-most column enter a "0" in each of the first 20 cells and a "1" in each of the next 20 cells[1]. In the next column (i.e., the Clothing column) enter a "0" in the first four cells, followed by a "1" in the next 16 cells, followed by a "0" in the next 13 cells, followed, finally, by a "1" in the next 7 cells. You should have data in cells 1–40.

Run the Analysis

Once the data are entered, go to Analyze, **Descriptive Statistics**, and Crosstabs. Transfer Country to the Row(s) box (it's conventional to have the **independent variable** in rows) and Clothing to the Column(s) box. Click Statistics, select Chi-square, and then click Continue. Click Cells, select Expected, Row, Column, and Total, then click Continue, then OK.

Interpret and Report the Results

Take a look at the Chi-Square Tests table. You're interested in the numbers in the top row (next to Pearson Chi-square); you'll need to refer to all three of the numbers when reporting the results. You can see that the **p-value** in the Asymp. **Sig.** (2-sided) column is below 0.05, so the result is **significant**. The percentages of people wearing t-shirts and jackets in the two countries are in the Country * Clothing Crosstabulation table; you should also refer to these when reporting (in APA format) the results:

Jackets were worn by a higher percentage people of people in Scotland (80%) compared to people in Spain (35%). A chi-squared test of independence revealed that jackets were worn significantly more often in Scotland than in Spain, χ^2 (1, $N = 40$) = 8.29[2], $p = .004$.

---

[1] If you have "Value Labels" selected in the View menu, the numbers you enter will be translated into descriptions of the **levels** of the variable. E.g., "0" will appear as "Scotland."

[2] According to APA guidelines, numbers should usually be rounded to two decimal places. However, this doesn't apply to **p-values**.

Thank you!

I would like to express my sincere thanks for your purchase of this guide!

If there's anything that you're still unsure about, please feel free to get in touch at DavidRobinson-Tutor@hotmail.com

If you found this guide useful, I would greatly appreciate if you could take a minute to leave a review on Amazon.

Wishing you the best of success,

David.

Glossary

Condition

Scientific experiments consist of multiple **conditions** – circumstances under which something is measured. For example, you could ask two groups of people how much they like pizza. One group could be hungry and the other not hungry. So, in this case, there are hungry and non-hungry **conditions**.

A more conventional experiment would be to assess whether a new medication is better at treating a disorder than a placebo (i.e., a "sugar pill" that doesn't contain the medication). In this case, there would be a control **condition**, in which participants receive the placebo, and a treatment **condition**, in which participants receive the new medication. The researcher would measure symptoms in both **conditions** before and after participants received the placebo or medication, which would allow them to determine the effectiveness of the treatment.

Covariate

Within the context of ANCOVAs and MANCOVAs, a **covariate** is a variable that might be related to a **dependent variable**, though is not the focus of the experiment (i.e., not the **independent variable**). It is necessary, therefore, to assess whether any observed relationships between independent and dependent variables are still evident after accounting for **covariates**. For instance, we could test whether a mathematics training programme improves mathematical ability. If there were two groups, one would undertake the mathematics training, and the other would complete training that was unrelated to mathematics. Subsequently, we would test mathematical ability, and we might see that those who completed the mathematics training had superior mathematical ability to those who did not. We might then conclude that the mathematics training was effective. However, it's possible that those who completed the mathematics training were simply better at mathematics before the training began. In this example, then, pre-training mathematical ability is a **covariate** that we should account for in order to better understand the relationship between type of training activity (the **independent variable**) and post-training mathematical ability (the **dependent variable**).

Degrees of freedom (df)

If I asked you to choose three numbers whose **mean** would equal 10, which would you choose? You might suggest 2, 6, and 22, or you might say 8, 12, and 10. The point is, there are many ways of getting there. However, once you had chosen 2 and 6, you no longer had any choice over the third number – it had to be 22. That is, the first two numbers were *free* to vary, though the third was not. So, in this situation, we have two **degrees of freedom**.

Similar situations occur when conducting statistical tests. For example, in the independent one-way ANOVA section, we imagined that there were three groups of cyclists – some went uphill, some downhill, and some flat. If we looked at *all* of the times taken to complete the courses – regardless of course type (uphill, downhill, flat) – we could calculate a grand **mean** (i.e., an overall **mean**). We could also calculate **means** for the different groups – we'll refer to these as cell **means**. If we knew two of the cell **means**, the third cell **mean** could only be one specific value given the grand **mean** (just like in the previous paragraph). One way of thinking about this situation is that two of the cell **means** were *free* to vary, while the third was not. This is why one of the **df** values in the example was 2.

Dependent variable

The **dependent variable** is the thing that's measured. For example, you could measure how many ice creams are sold at a café on sunny days vs. rainy days. In this situation, the **independent variable** would be the weather and the **dependent variable** would be the number of ice creams sold.

For a more serious example, imagine that researchers want to investigate whether a new drug improves learning. They give one group the drug and another group a placebo (i.e., a "sugar pill" that doesn't contain the drug). They give the participants an hour to read an article, then give them a quiz about it. In this case, their score on the quiz is the **dependent variable**.

Descriptive statistics

As the name implies, **descriptive statistics** merely describe the data; they are *not* used to make inferences about, for example, whether a difference between groups should be deemed **significant** (for this, **inferential statistics** are employed). Common **descriptive statistics** include "measures of central tendency" – **means**, medians, and modes. However, **descriptive statistics** can also describe how dispersed the data are (e.g., **standard deviation)** or might simply indicate how many participants are in a sample.

F-value (F statistic)

Essentially, this value reflects the extent to which variation in the **dependent variable** (DV) can be attributed to variation in the **independent variable** (IV). Therefore, high values suggest that the IV has a strong impact on the DV.

Independent/between samples/measures/participants

Independent designs involve having *separate* participants in different **conditions**. For example, you might want to determine whether some musicians are better singers than others. You could recruit guitarists, pianists, and violinists and have them complete a singing exam. None of the musicians would be able to play either of the two instruments of the groups to which they do not belong (e.g., guitarists couldn't also play the piano or the violin). Independent designs contrast with **paired designs**, which entail one group of participants being assessed in multiple **conditions**.

Independent variable

In experiments, the **independent variable** is the thing that is manipulated, which allows researchers to measure its influence on a **dependent variable**. For instance, you could test whether participants can type faster before or after caffeine; you would simply give one group regular coffee and one group decaffeinated coffee and have them complete a typing test. In this case, the **independent variable** is coffee type (regular or decaff), while the **dependent variable** – the thing that you measure – is the number of words typed in a given amount of time.

Inferential statistics

Inferential statistical tests are the foundation of this guide (e.g., t-tests, ANOVAs, ANCOVAs). Experiments in psychology usually consist of a sample of participants and we assume that this sample is representative of the wider population. Inferential tests, therefore, allow us to *infer* whether our observations of a sample can be extended to the population. The crucial difference between **descriptive statistics** and inferential statistics within the context of this book is that the latter allow us to investigate **statistical significance**. For instance, if we see that participants in one **condition** obtain higher scores on a test than participants in another, we can use **inferential statistics** to determine the likelihood of such a difference occurring by chance.

Interaction effect

In its most basic form, an **interaction effect** is apparent when the influence of one **independent variable** (IV) on a **dependent variable** (DV) is influenced by variation in another IV. For instance, let's imagine that there are two running races, each with a unique prize – either a new bike or a new surfboard for the winner. Let's also suppose that half of the participants are keen cyclists, while the other are keen surfers. We want to know how the prize and the participants' interests (cycling or surfing) affect race times. So, the prize and the participants' interests are the two IVs, while race times are the DV. The results might indicate that, *overall*, neither of the IVs **significantly** affect race times (this outcome assumes that both groups of participants are equally good runners and that, overall, the prizes represent comparable incentives). However, it's conceivable that the cyclists would be faster when the prize is a bike, while the surfers would be faster when the prize is a surfboard.

Thus, the influence of one IV (participants' interests) on race times, depends upon variation in the other IV (prize).

Level

Levels are the constituents of **nominal/categorical variables**. For example, a psychologist might be interested in the effectiveness of three different treatments on a disorder, such as anxiety. Participants with anxiety would be allocated to one of three groups – let's say these are cognitive behavioural therapy, benzodiazepines (drugs), or exercise. In this instance, "treatment" is the **independent variable (IV)** and the three aforementioned treatments are the **levels** within the IV.

Linear relationship/association

A **linear relationship** means that an increase of a given size in one variable (i.e., one unit) is *consistently* associated with an increase or decrease of a *specific* size in another variable. This relationship could be represented by a *straight* line on a graph (see below).

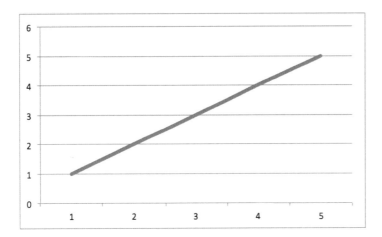

For example, imagine you're driving a new car along a road at a fixed speed, say 50 miles per hour. You look at the milometer after an hour and it says that you've driven 50 miles, and you look at it after two hours and it says you've driven 100 miles, and so forth. If you created a graph where time was on the x-axis and distance was on the y-axis and you entered the data from your drive, the points could be joined by a straight *line* – hence the name *line*ar. With every hour, distance increases in a *consistent* manner (+ 50 miles).

Mean (aka "average")

The **mean** is calculated by adding together values and dividing by the number of values. For instance, a researcher might be interested in how many calories are consumed per day by people in one country versus another, such as the USA and India. The researcher recruits three participants from each country. The three from the USA consume 3600, 4000, and 3800 each per day; the three from India consume 2400, 2200, and 2600 each per day. Therefore, to calculate the number of calories consumed by the participants in the USA, first add up the appropriate values: 3600 + 4000 + 3800 = 11400. If you divide this value by three you get a **mean** of 3800. The same process can be used to determine the **mean** for the Indian sample, which is 2400. You can also calculate the grand **mean**, which, in this case, is the **mean** number of calories consumed by participants regardless of country. This could be done by adding all of the six original values and then dividing by six. However, since we already know the two group **means**, these can simply be added together and divided by two: 3800 + 2400/2 = 3100.

Negative correlation

This refers to instances in which an increase in one variable is associated with a decrease in another variable. For example, you could look at how many cloudy days there are per year in different countries and ask whether this correlates with how many bottles of sun cream are purchased per year in those countries. One might expect that increased cloudiness would be associated with decreased sun cream sales. In which case, if the number of cloudy days were represented on the x-axis of a graph and the number of bottles of sun cream sold were represented on the y-axis, you would expect the data points to congregate around a line of best fit that is high towards the left of the graph and low towards the right (see below).

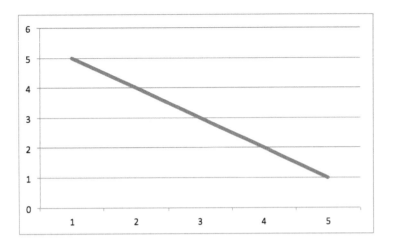

A **nominal** or **categorical variable** is simply one that consists of groups. You might want to investigate whether meditation enhances happiness, so you allocate some participants to a meditation group and some to a control group. You could give them a questionnaire that assesses happiness at the beginning of the experiment and one at the end, maybe several months later. In this case, the **categorical variable** could be named "Treatment," and it would consist of two groups or **levels** – meditation or no meditation.

Ordinal data

Questionnaires, for example, generally produce **ordinal data**. For instance, a researcher might ask participants to indicate the extent to which they agree with a statement; they might have to choose between: strongly disagree, disagree, neither agree nor disagree, agree, and strongly agree. In order to translate responses into numerical data, the researcher might consider a "strongly disagree" response to be equal to zero, while a "disagree" response would equal one, and so forth. These numbers could then be entered into a spreadsheet or SPSS. As the name implies, **ordinal data** can be *ordered*. That is, if one person says that they "agree" with a statement, while another says that they "strongly agree," you know which one agrees with the statement more. However, it's not possible to really know *how much* more the second person agrees with the statement; it would sound strange to say that they agreed "1" more than the first person! In this respect, **ordinal data** differ from **scale data**, for which the differences between units are precise and meaningful.

Paired/repeated samples/measures/participants

This is a type of experimental design. Specifically, it is one that involves individual groups of participants experiencing multiple **conditions**. For instance, you might be interested in whether students' mathematical abilities are better in the morning or the afternoon. To investigate this, you give a group of students a maths test in the morning and the same group a different maths test of equal difficulty in the afternoon. You then compare results (probably with a paired t-test). The **independent-** or **between-participants** version of this experiment would have two groups of students – one that takes the morning test, and one that takes the afternoon test.

Positive correlation

Unsurprisingly, a **positive correlation** is the opposite of a **negative correlation**. A **positive correlation** refers to instances in which an increase in one variable is associated with an increase in another variable. For example, you might predict that height is **positively correlated** with weight. Although there are tall, light people and short, heavy people, it's reasonable to assume that, generally speaking, tall people are heavier. You could measure the height and weight of, say, 50 people and then plot the data on a graph, with height on the x-axis and weight on the y-axis. If there were a **positive correlation** between the two variables, you would expect the data points to congregate around a line of best fit that extends from the bottom left to the top right of the graph (see below).

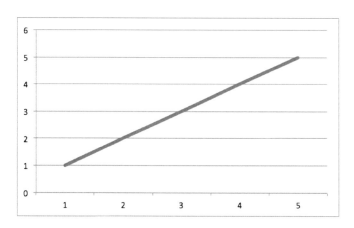

P-Value/Sig value

A **p-value** is indication of how likely a result is. For example, we could investigate whether people who live by the sea are better swimmers than those who don't. To test this, it would just be a matter of recruiting, say, 10 people who live by the coast and 10 that don't, and then have them swim a length of a pool as fast as they can. When we look at the times, we might see that those who live by the sea tend to be faster. However, this might just be a coincidence. With this particular experiment, we could conduct an independent t-test, which would give us a **p-value**. If the value were, say, 0.04, what would we conclude? Well, since it's below 0.05, we would consider the result **significant**. A value of 0.04 indicates that there's only a 4% chance that a difference in times of the observed size would occur just by chance (i.e., that participants who live by the sea simply happen to be that much faster).

Scale data

Like **ordinal data**, there's an inherent order to **scale data**. That is, a given value is clearly higher, lower, or the same as another value. However, unlike **ordinal data**, there are precise differences between units. Imagine there're a javelin competition; one athlete throws their javelin 80 metres, while another throws theirs 87 metres. In this situation, it's obvious that the second athlete threw theirs further and that there's an exact difference between the two distances – 7 metres.

Standard deviation

A **standard deviation** is an indication of how spread out the data are. To calculate it, you determine the square root of variance. Variance is the **average** of squared differences from the **mean**. This isn't as complicated as it might sound. Suppose we want to get a feel for how much variation there is in height within a group of three people. Participant 1 is 150 cm, Participant 2 is 165 cm, and Participant 3 is 195 cm. Their **mean** height is their combined height divided by the number of participants: 510 cm/3 = 170 cm. Next, we determine squared differences from the **mean** by subtracting the **mean** from each of the individual heights and squaring the answers. 150 cm – 170 cm = -20cm, which, when squared is 400 cm. 165 cm – 170 cm = -5 cm, which, when squared is 25 cm. 195 cm – 170 cm = 25 cm, which when squared is 625 cm. To determine the sum of squared differences from the **mean**, we add these results together: 400 cm + 25 cm + 625 cm = 1050 cm. The **average** of squared differences from the **mean** (i.e., the variance), then, is 1050 cm divided by 3, which is 350 cm. To calculate the **standard deviation**, you determine the square root of the variance, which, in this case is about 19 cm. We can now refer to individuals as being within or outside of a certain number of **standard deviations** from the **mean**. One **standard deviation** above the **mean** is 189 cm (170 cm + 19 cm) and one **standard deviation** below is 151 cm (170 cm – 19 cm). Therefore, only Participant 2 is within one **standard deviation** of the **mean**. Note that this statistic is referred to as a **"standard" deviation** because it could be applied to any type of unit. In this example, we used cm, but we could have substituted cm for metres and pretended that we were analysing a small group of giants. Either way, only the giant version of Participant 2, at 165 *metres* tall, would be within one **standard deviation** from the **mean**.

Statistical significance

A statistically **significant** result is one that is unlikely to be due to random variation. A researcher might be interested in how different types of music affect how people feel. For example, they might ask whether classical music or heavy metal is better for instilling a sense of calmness. To test this, they have one group of participants listen to classical music and another group of participants listen to heavy metal. After, the participants complete a questionnaire about how calm they feel. Suppose that those in the classical music **condition** have higher calmness scores than those in the heavy metal **condition**, how do we know whether this difference is **significant**. With this **independent samples** design, the researcher could conduct an independent t-test, which would provide them with a **p-value**. If the value were below 0.05, they could say that there was a **significant** effect of music type on calmness. You might ask: if we can see that the calmness scores are higher in the classical music **condition**, why conduct the t-test? The answer is that there will be natural variations in calmness (i.e., some people are simply more calm than others). Without conducting the test, it remains a possibility that the difference in calmness scores between groups exists simply because calmer people just happened to be allocated to the classical music **condition**.

In fact, however, a **p-value** of 0.05 doesn't rule out this possibility, it just indicates that there's only a 5% chance of this being the case. You might also ask: why do we consider **p-values** that are below 0.05 **significant**? Well, it's essentially an arbitrary cut-off point.

Made in the USA
Monee, IL
19 February 2023

28166191R00036